SPOTLIGHT on MUSIC ™

Authors

Judy Bond

René Boyer

Margaret Campbelle-Holman

Emily Crocker

Marilyn C. Davidson

Robert de Frece

Virginia Ebinger

Mary Goetze

Betsy M. Henderson

John Jacobson

Michael Jothen

Chris Judah-Lauder

Carol King

Vincent P. Lawrence

Ellen McCullough-Brabson

Janet McMillion

Nancy L. T. Miller

Ivy Rawlins

Susan Snyder

Gilberto D. Soto

Kodály Contributing Consultant

Sr. Lorna Zemke

HAL•LEONARD®

McGraw Hill Macmillan McGraw-Hill

i

ACKNOWLEDGMENTS

Creative Direction and Delivery: The Quarasan Group, Inc.

The Broadway Junior® logo and MTI® logo are trademarks of Music Theatre International. All rights reserved.

Grateful acknowledgment is given to the following authors, composers, and publishers. Every effort has been made to trace the ownership of all copyrighted material and to secure the necessary permissions to reprint these selections. In the case of some selections for which acknowledgment is not given, extensive research has failed to locate the copyright holders.

Songs and Speech Pieces

Big and Small, by Ellen McCullough Brabson. Used by Permission.

Double This, Collected from Tyler Samuel, Ayana Cousin and Allyssa Cousin, by Margaret Campbelle-Holman. Copyright © 2002. Benchmark Press, LLC. International copyright secured. All Rights Reserved.

Hunt the Cows, Scandinavian Singing Game. Words by Jean Ritchie. Copyright © 1968 (Renewed 1996) by Jean Ritchie/Geordie Music Publishing Co. International Copyright Secured. All Rights Reserved. Used by Permission.

Kari (Wild Geese), from *Children's Songs From Japan.* Japanese Folk Song. English Words by Florence White and Kazuo Akiyama. Copyright © 1960 by Edward B. Marks Music Company. Copyright Renewed. International Copyright Secured. All Rights Reserved. Used by Permission.

Little Black Bug, Words by Margaret Wise Brown. Music by Ruth Boshkoff. From *All Around the Buttercup: Early Experiences With Orff Schulwerk,* edited by Ruth Boshkoff. Copyright © 1984 Schott Music Corp. All Rights Reserved.

Mary's Coal Black Lamb, American Song. Words by Ken Foy. Copyright © 1993 by Alfred Publishing Co., Inc. International Copyright Secured. All Rights Reserved. Used by Permission.

Na Bahia Tem (In Bahia Town), from *90 Songs of the Americas Compiled and Arranged by Ruth DeCesare.* © 1993 EMI MILLS MUSIC, INC. Worldwide Print Rights on behalf of EMI MILLS MUSIC, INC. Administered by WARNER BROS. PUBLICATIONS U.S. INC. All Rights Reserved. Used by Permission.

Serra, serra serrador (Saw, Saw Lumberjack), from *Roots & Branches.* Brazilian Counting Song. Copyright © World Music Press (ASCAP). World Music Press, P.O. Box 2565, Danbury, CT 06813-2565, www.worldmusicpress.com. All Rights Reserved.

Step into the Spotlight, Words and Music by Emily Crocker, John Higgins and John Jacobson. Copyright © 2004 by HAL LEONARD CORPORATION. International Copyright Secured. All Rights Reserved.

When the Flag Goes By, Words and Music by Lynn Freeman Olson. Copyright © 1985 by Alfred Publishing Co., Inc. International Copyright Secured. All Rights Reserved. Used by Permission.

Yo, Mamana, Yo (Oh, Mama, Oh), from *Roots & Branches.* Shanganan Folk Song. Copyright © World Music Press (ASCAP). World Music Press, P.O. Box 2565, Danbury, CT 06813-2565, www.worldmusicpress.com. All Rights Reserved.

(Continued on page 155.)   A

The **McGraw·Hill** Companies

 Macmillan/McGraw-Hill

Published by Macmillan/McGraw-Hill, of McGraw-Hill Education, a division of The McGraw-Hill Companies, Inc., Two Penn Plaza, New York, New York 10121.

ISBN: 978-0-02-296697-3
MHID: 0-02-296697-8

1 2 3 4 5 6 7 8 9 RJE 16 15 14 13 12 11 10   Printed in the United States of America

CONTRIBUTORS

Consultants

Brian Burnett,
Movement

Stephen Gabriel,
Technology

Magali Iglesias,
English Language Learners

Roberta Newcomer,
Special Learners/Assessment

Frank Rodríguez,
English Language Learners

Jacque Schrader,
Movement

Kathy B. Sorensen,
International Phonetic
Alphabet

Patti Windes-Bridges,
Listening Maps

Linda Worsley,
Listening/Singable
English Translations

Sr. Lorna Zemke,
Kodály Contributing
Consultant

Recordings

Executive Producer: John Higgins
Senior Music Editor/Producer: Emily Crocker
Senior Recording Producer: Mark Brymer
Recording Producers: Steve Millikan, Andy Waterman
Associate Recording Producers: Alan Billingsley, Darrell Bledsoe, Stacy Carson, Rosanna Eckert, John Egan, Chad Evans, Darlene Koldenhoven, Chris Koszuta, Don Markese, Matthew McGregor, Steve Potts, Edwin Schupman, Michael Spresser, Frank Stegall, David Vartanian, Mike Wilson, Ted Wilson
Project/Mastering Engineer: Mark Aspinall; Post-Production Engineer: Don Sternecker

Selected recordings by Buryl Red, Executive Producer; Michael Rafter, Senior Recording Producer; Bryan Louiselle and Buddy Skipper, Recording Producers; Lori Casteel and Mick Rossi, Associate Recording Producers; Jonathan Duckett, Supervising Engineer

Contributing Writers

Allison Abucewicz, Sharon Berndt, Rhona Brink, Ann Burbridge, Debbie Helm Daniel, Katherine Domingo, Kari Gilbertson, Janet Graham, Hilree Hamilton, Linda Harley, Judy Henneberger, Carol Huffman, Bernie Hynson, Jr., Sheila A. Kerley, Elizabeth Kipperman, Ellen Mendelsohn, Cristi Cary Miller, Leigh Ann Mock, Patricia O'Rourke, Barbara Resch, Soojin Kim Ritterling, Isabel Romero, Carl B. Schmidt, Debra Shearer, Ellen Mundy Shuler, Rebecca Treadway, Carol Wheeler, Sheila Woodward

Multicultural Consultants

William Anderson, Chet-Yeng Loong, Edwin Schupman, Kathy B. Sorensen, Gilberto D. Soto, Judith Cook Tucker, Dennis Waring

In the Spotlight Consultant

Willa Dunleavy

Multicultural Advisors

Brad Ahawanrathe Bonaparte (Mohawk), Emmanuel Akakpo (Ewe), Earlene Albano (Hawaiian), Luana Au (Maori), Bryan Ayakawa (Japanese), Ruby Beeston (Mandarin), Latif Bolat (Turkish), Estella Christensen (Spanish), Oussama Davis (Arabic), Mia Delguardo (Minahasa), Nolutho Ndengane Diko (Xhosa), Angela Fields (Hopi, Chemehuevi), Gary Fields (Lakota, Cree), Gilad Harel (Hebrew), Josephine Hetarihon (Bahasa Indonesian, Minahasa, and Maluko dialect), Judy Hirt-Manheimer (Hebrew), Rose Jakub (Navajo), Elizabeth Jarema (Fijian), Rita Jensen (Swedish), Malou Jewett (Visayan), Alejandro Jimenez (Hispanic), Chris Jones (Hungarian), Wendy Jyang Shamo (Mandarin), Amir Kalay (Hebrew), Michael Katsan (Greek), Silvi Madarajan (Tamil), Georgia Magpie (Comanche), Nona Mardi (Malay), Aida Mattingly (Tagalog), Mike Kanathohare McDonald (Mohawk), Vasana de Mel (Sinhala), Marion Miller (Czech), Etsuko Miskin (Japanese), Mogens Mogenson (Danish), Kenny Tahawisoren Perkins (Mohawk), Pradeep Nayyar (Punjabi, Hindi), Renu Nayyar (Punjabi), Mfanego Ngwenya (Zulu), Wil Numkena (Hopi), Samuel Owuru (Akan), Nina Padukone (Konkani), Hung Yong Park (Korean), James Parker (Finnish), Jose Pereira (Konkani), Berrit Price (Norwegian), John Rainer (Taos Pueblo, Creek), Lillian Rainer (Taos Pueblo, Creek, Apache), Arnold Richardson (Haliwa-Saponi), Ken Runnacles (German), Trudy Shenk (German), Ron Singer (Navajo), Ernest Siva (Cahuilla, Serrano [Maringa']), Bonnie Slade (Swedish), Cristina Sorrentino (Portuguese), Diane Thram (Xhosa), Elena Todorov (Bulgarian), Zlatina Todorov (Russian), Tom Toronto (Lao, Thai), Rebecca Wilberg (French, Italian), Sheila Woodward (Zulu), Keith Yackeyonny (Comanche)

Contents

Spotlight on Music Reading.............78

Spotlight on Performance............104

Spotlight on Celebrations..........122

In the Spotlight

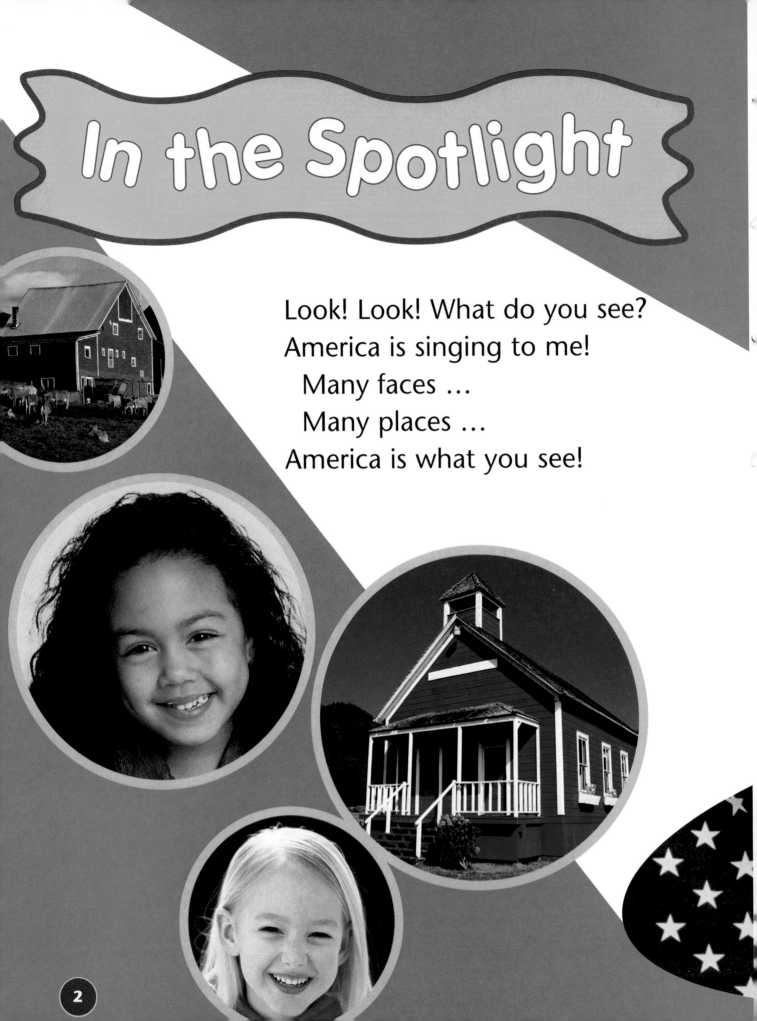

Look! Look! What do you see?
America is singing to me!
Many faces …
Many places …
America is what you see!

A bright light shines on America!

What Do You Hear?

Listen! Listen!
Do you hear a sound?
I hear music all around.
Is it a river?
Is it a train?
Is it a city?
Is it rain?

Share the Spotlight

Do you see a light?
The light is so bright!
Just look! Do you see?
It shines for you and me!

Step into the Spotlight

 **Spotlight CD**
Track 1

Come on and step into the spotlight!
Let it shine, shine, shine
on our music and our song.

Spotlight on America

Where in the world can we be?
The bright light shines on you and me.
We sing out loud.
We stand so proud.
America is the bright light I see!

Patriotic Medley

 **Spotlight CD
Track 4**

You're a Grand Old Flag
This Land Is Your Land
America the Beautiful

Spotlight on Concepts

Spotlight on Concepts

Long and Short

Where do you hear a **steady beat**?

CD 1:12

WILLUM

Music gets higher as it moves **upward**.

Music gets lower as it moves **downward**.

Make your voice go upward or downward.

Follow "Willum" as it goes up and down.

Steady Beat

CD 1:15 **The Ants Go Marching**

Your heart beats with a steady beat.
You can march with a steady beat.

Tap each ant with a steady beat as you sing.

"The Royal March of the Lions"
by Camille Saint-Saëns

Keep the beat!
Move like these animals.

Art Gallery

The Peaceable Kingdom
by Edward Hicks

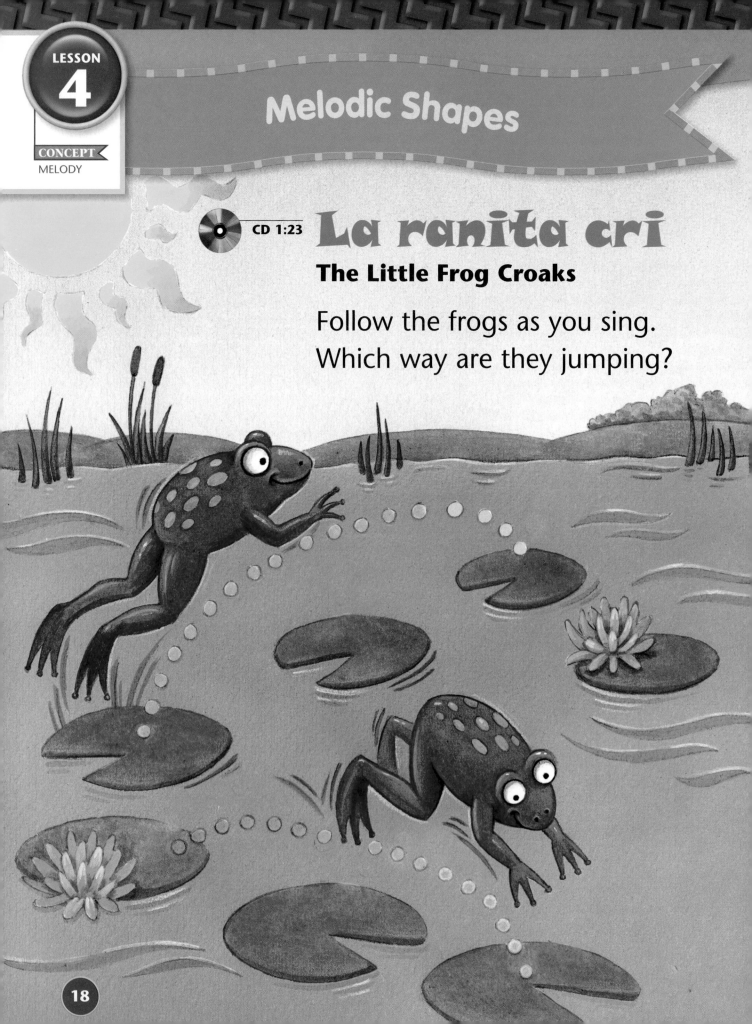

CD 1:23

La ranita cri

The Little Frog Croaks

Follow the frogs as you sing.
Which way are they jumping?

Squiggle Sounds

Match these shapes with your voice!

Make up your own squiggle sounds with your voice.

Louder and Softer

The sign for softer sounds is *p*.

The sign for louder sounds is *f*.

Follow the map as you listen to "March."

LISTENING CD 1:27

March by Georges Bizet

Listening Map for March

getting softer!

very soft

How would you say this poem? How would you use **p** or **f**?

Rain Poem

Rain	on the	green	grass
Rain	on the	tree	
Rain	on the	hill-	top but
Not	on	me!	

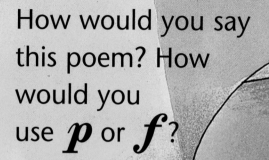

🎨 Art Gallery

Paris Street; Rainy Day
by Gustave Caillebotte

This is a street in France. Does it look like a street in your town?

Long and Short

Long

Short

Look at the picture.

What makes a **long** sound?
What makes a **short** sound?

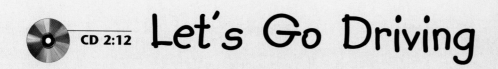

Let's Go Driving

Music has long sounds and short sounds.

Listen for long sounds in the song.

High and Low

Some sounds are **high**.
Some sounds are **low**.

Make your voice move
high and low as you sing
"Hoo, Hoo!"

CD 2:21 Hoo, Hoo!

Hoo!

Hoo!

24

Look at the pictures.

Can you hear high and low sounds?

Show high by touching your shoulders.
Show low by touching your waist.

Hoo!

Hoo!

Longer and Shorter

Say "splash" for

Say "pitter, patter" for

Which sounds were longer?
Which sounds were shorter?

Duérmete mi niño
Go to Sleep, My Baby

CD 2:28

Listen to the song.
Follow the longer and
shorter sounds.

Higher and Lower

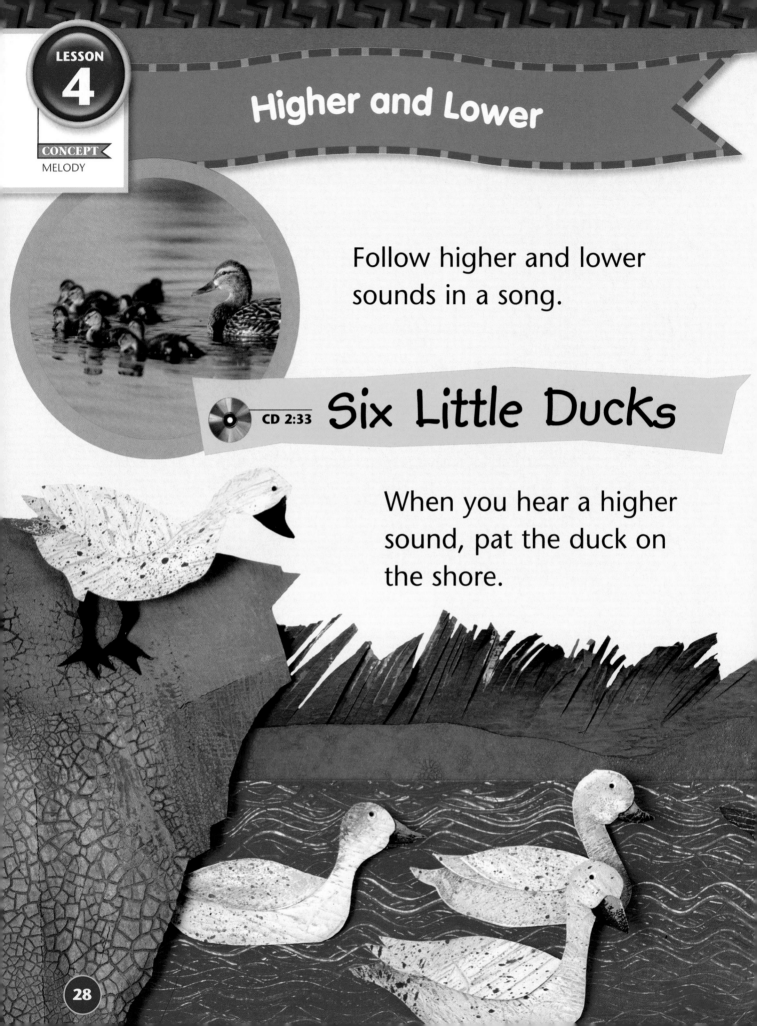

Follow higher and lower sounds in a song.

CD 2:33 **Six Little Ducks**

When you hear a higher sound, pat the duck on the shore.

Flute and Tuba

The **flute** makes higher sounds.

The **tuba** makes lower sounds.

flute

When you hear a higher sound, pat the flute.
When you hear a lower sound, pat the tuba.

tuba

Ways to Use Your Voice

Sing and speak to play this game.

CD 2:40

Sara
Watashi

Plate
Passing

Open your eyes!
Who has the plate?

singing

speaking

whispering

calling

What voices will you use today?
When will you use each voice?

Navajo Rhythms

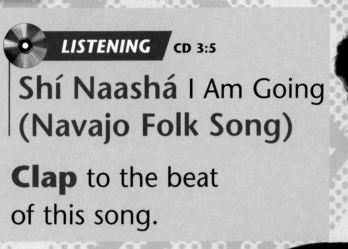

LISTENING CD 3:5

Shí Naashá I Am Going
(Navajo Folk Song)

Clap to the beat
of this song.

Navajo drum

Marilyn Help is a
Navajo teacher.
She sings Navajo
songs.

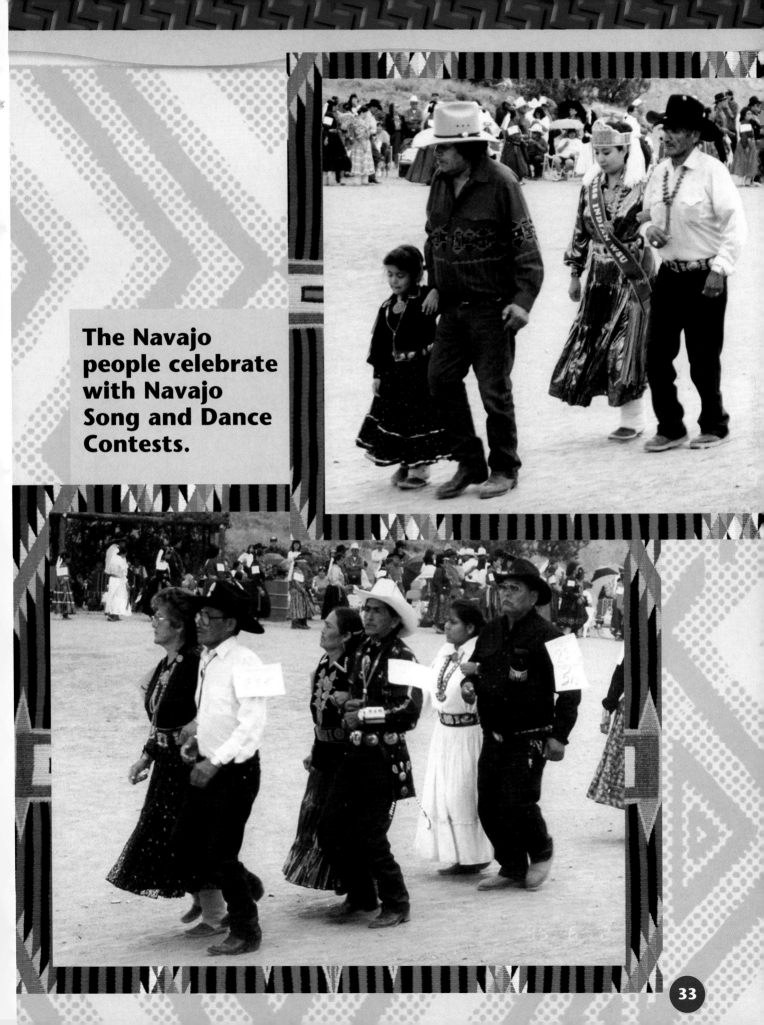

The Navajo people celebrate with Navajo Song and Dance Contests.

Rhythm

But the Critter Got Away

CD 3:29

"Who's been eating up my corn?"
Cried the farmer one fine morn.
"Saw a rabbit, tried to grab it,
But the critter got away."

Say and clap these words.

corn   **crit-ter**

Which word has one sound with the beat?
Which word has two sounds with the beat?

Clap these words.

crit-ter   crit-ter   crit-ter   corn

The way the words go is called **rhythm**.

Play Rhythms

Mar-co **dance**

Which word has one sound on the beat?
Which word has two sounds?

Marco Polo

CD 3:35

Marco Polo went to France,
Taught the ladies how to dance.
First a kick, then a bow,
Marco Polo showed them how.

woods **metals** **scrapers and shakers** **drums**

Gavotte
by Sergei Prokofiev

Play along with "Gavotte."

Listening Map for Gavotte

 Steady beat

 Play three times.

Play one time.

 Steady beat

 CD 4:4

Double This

Double   this   that

Read and play the game.

Dou-ble	dou-ble	this	this
Dou-ble	dou-ble	that	that
Dou-ble	this	dou-ble	that
Dou-ble	dou-ble	this	that

You can show one
sound to a beat with ♩

You can show two
sounds to a beat with ♫

Clap the rhythm.

Dou-ble = 2 sounds ♫

this = 1 sound ♩

Clap and read.

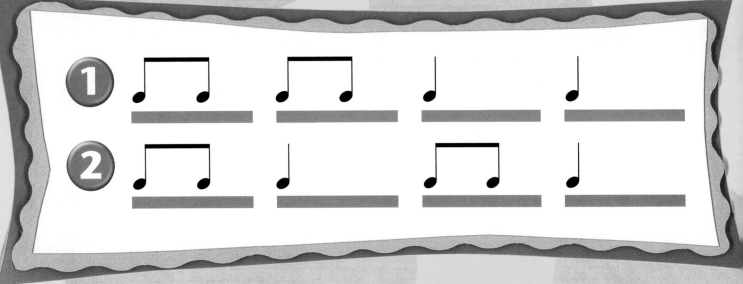

Match each line of "Double
This" with a rhythm above.

Rhythm of the Words

Quaker, Quaker

CD 4:17

American Folk Song

"Quak - er, Quak - er, how is thee?"

"Ver - y well, I thank thee."

"How's thy neigh - bor next to thee?"

"I don't know, I'll go and see."

eighth notes

Quak-er

quarter note

see

Match each line of "Quaker, Quaker" with one of these rhythms.

Play the rhythm patterns on a drum.

Changing Rhythms

Granny

CD 4:28

Traditional

"Gran-ny, will your dog bite,

Cow kick, cat scratch?

Gran-ny, will your hen peck?"

"No, child, no."

El juego chirimbolo

The Chirimbolo Game

 CD 4:24

Adapted and Arranged
by Elizabeth Villarreal Brennan

(Spanish)
El juego chirimbolo,
  que bonito es,
Con un pie, otro pie,
Una mano, otra mano,
Un codo, otro codo.

The game of Chirimbolo,
what a lot of fun!
With one foot, other foot,
with a hand, other hand,
an elbow, other elbow.

43

Higher and Lower

 CD 5:23 I've a Pair of Fishes

Listen for higher and lower **pitches** with these rhyming words.

Touch your shoulders for higher pitches.
Touch your waist for lower pitches.

fish-es   fish-es   dish-es   dish-es

pup-pies   pup-pies   gup-pies   gup-pies

Say the rhythm.
Clap the rhythm.

CD 5:20 One, Two, Three, Four

Traditional

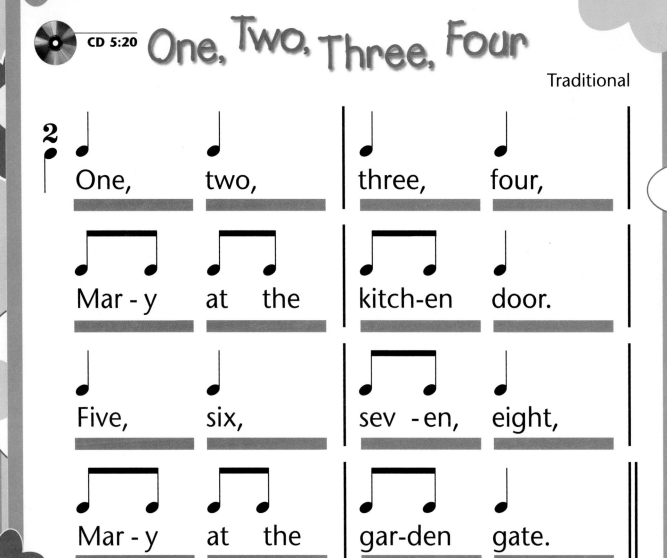

Faster and Slower

Some music goes fast.
Some music goes slow.

 LISTENING CD 6:2

December: Sleighride
by Judith Lang Zaimont

Listening Map for December: Sleighride

LISTENING CD 6:1

Andante
by Franz Joseph Haydn

Listening Map for Andante

A Part 1 and Part 3

B Part 2

 LISTENING CD 6:3

Singing on the Fisherboats at Dusk (Chinese Folk Song)

So and *Mi*

Higher and lower pitches can be written on a **staff** . *So* is higher. *Mi* is lower.

When *so* is in a space, *mi* is in the space below.

so   Tin - ker,   tail - or,   sol - dier,   sail - or,

CD 6:4

Tinker, Tailor

Traditional

so   Tin - ker,   tail - or,   sol - dier,   sail - or,

Rich man,   poor man,   beg-gar man,   thief.

When *so* is on a line,
mi is on the line below.

Serra, serra serrador

Saw, Saw Lumberjack

CD 6:7

Brazilian Counting Song
English words by Emily Crocker

Portuguese: **Ser - ra,   ser - ra,   ser - ra - dor.**
English: **Saw - ing,   saw - ing, lum - ber - jack.**

Quan - tos   paus o se-nhor   ser - ron?
How many   logs_____ will   you   stack?

49

Louder and Softer

These are **repeat** signs. 𝄆 𝄇
Repeat everything inside them.

Come Back, My Little Chicks

CD 6:11

Hungarian Children's Game
Adapted by Rhona Brink

Leader

Come back home, my   lit - tle chicks.

Group   *Leader*

We   won't come.   Why   not?
We're   a - fraid.   Of   what?

Group   *Leader*

Of   the wolf.   Where's he   hid - ing?
In   the woods. What's he   do - ing?

How will you sing this song?
Will you sing loud or soft?
Will you sing fast or slow?

Group   *Leader*

Wash - ing.   Where's he   wash - ing?

Group   *Leader*

By   the   stream.   What's he   dry   his

Group

face   on?   On the kit - ty   cat's   tail!

Story and Sound

🔘 **LISTENING** CD 6:19

Peter and the Wolf
by Sergei Prokofiev

Tap each instrument when you hear it.

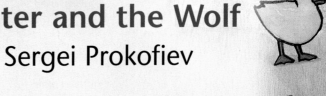

violin

flute

oboe

clarinet

bassoon

timpani

French horn

Same and Different

LISTENING CD 6:20

Music from Bali (Gamelan Ensemble)

Which instruments
are the same?

Which are different?

**Gamelan Music
from Bali**

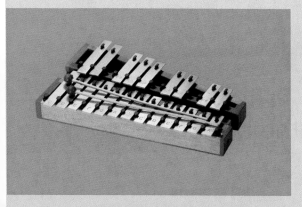

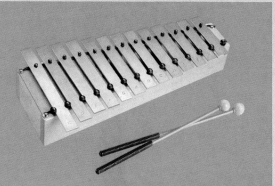

Pat Works on the Railway (Orff version)

Each musical instrument has its own sound.

Listen to these instruments.

A Beat with No Sound

Some music has sound on the beat.
Some music has no sound on the beat.

Johnny's Flea

CD 7:10

One,   two,   three,

John-ny caught a flea.

Flea   died,   John-ny cried,

Tee,   hee,   hee.

Tee, hee, hee

In My Little Motor Boat

 CD 7:13

Putt-putt, putt-putt, putt-putt, putt-putt,

In my lit - tle mo - tor boat,

Putt-putt, putt-putt, putt-putt, putt-putt,

Hear the en - gine go!

Which beats have 2 sounds?
Which beats have 1 sound?
Which beat has no sound?

Read and **clap** the motor boat pattern.
Move your hands apart to show
the beat with no sound.

A New Pitch

Sing these words.

Show the melodic direction with your hands and voice.

Find the new pitch.

Flea   John-ny
....died........   cried

        ly
Lit-tle   Walk-
        Sal-   er

I   spin-
    like
                ach

The new pitch has its own place.

Where is the new pitch?

so

Point to the pictures. **Describe** the melodic direction of songs you know.

mi

Read a Rest!

Read and clap this line.
Find the beat with no sound.

Lit-tle   black   bug,   Lit-tle   black   bug,

One sound on a beat
is called a quarter note.

Two sounds on a beat are
called two eighth notes.

A beat with no sound is
called a **rest**.

Find the rests in this song.
Read and **clap** each line.
Sing the song.

Little Black Bug

CD 7:22

Words by Margaret Wise Brown
Music by Ruth Boshkoff

Lit - tle black bug, Lit - tle black bug,

where have you been? "I've been un - der the rug,"

said the lit - tle black bug. "Bug, ugh, ugh."

61

Mi, So, La

You know *so* and *mi*. The new pitch
is called *la.* Sing these pitches.

so   la   so   mi

Which pitch is highest?
Which pitch is in the middle?
Which pitch is lowest?

 CD 7:34   Naughty Kitty Cat

Name and sing these pitches.
Listen for this pattern in the song.

Find this pattern in "Twenty-four Robbers."

Beats in Groups of Twos and Threes

Beats can be grouped together.
Each jewel shows a beat.
How many beats are grouped
together on each crown?

 LISTENING CD 8:7

Minuet by Henry Purcell

Art Gallery

Detail of *The Coronation of Emperor Napoleon I Bonaparte and Empress Josephine* by Jacques Louis David

This painting shows a queen being crowned.

How are the beats grouped in these crowns?

Choose two pitched instruments.

Play a lower pitch for red jewels.

Play a higher pitch for purple jewels.

![CD] **LISTENING** CD 8:11

Promenade
by Linda Worsley

AB Form

LA CAMILLA  CD 9:5

Fiesta Dance

Some music has two parts.
The first part is called Ⓐ.
The second part is called Ⓑ.

A

Move like this when
you hear the A part.

B

Move like this when
you hear the B part.

The Well of Toledo by Diego Rivera

How many groups are in this picture?

Rhythm: Read and Play

Clap and **read** this speech piece.

 CD 9:13

BIG AND SMALL

Ellen McCullough Brabson

2

El - e - phants are big,

Spi - ders are small.

How can a spi - der's web

Hold them all?

A Say the poem for your A part.

B **Sing** "One Little Elephant" for your B part.

Decide how many times to do each part.

69

ABA Form

 LISTENING CD 9:20

The Elephant
by Camille Saint-Saëns

"The Elephant"
has three parts:
Ⓐ Ⓑ Ⓐ.

Listening Map for The Elephant

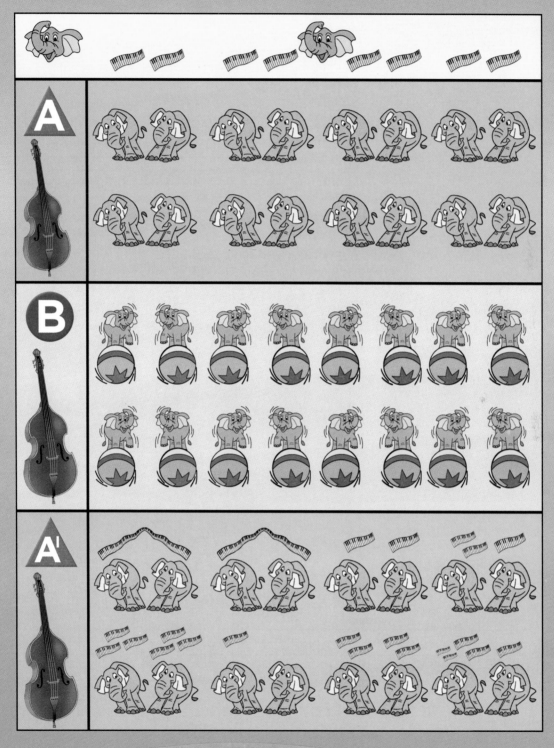

Create Melodies

CONCEPT
MELODY

Read this song using pitches you know: *mi*, *so*, and *la*.

If *so* is on a line, *mi* is on the line below. *La* is in the space above *so*.

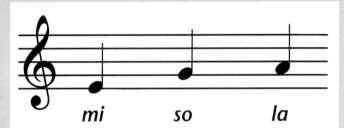

Little Robin Red Breast

CD 9:21

English Rhyme

Lit - tle Rob - in Red Breast came to vis - it me.

This is what he whis - tled: "Thank you for my tea."

72

Write a melody using *mi*, *so*, and *la*.

Hear Instruments

Mai Nozipo by Dumisani Maraire

mbira

hosho

ngoma

Listen to these African instruments.

Dumisani Maraire

74

Listen to these string instruments.

2 violins

1 viola

1 cello

Four string instruments form a string quartet.

Create Rhythms

Punchinella  CD 10:1

Play these patterns with the song.
Choose an instrument to play
each pattern.

Old King Glory

CD 10:4

Make up your own patterns to play with this song. Which instrument will you choose?

claves

triangle

drum

shaker

Spotlight on
Music Reading

Spotlight on Music Reading

Keep the Beat

Sing and tap the hands.

 CD 10:17

Hello, There!

 CD 10:20

Jambo

Hello

 **LISTENING** CD 10:23

Trumpet and Drum
by Georges Bizet

Listen and tap the trumpets
and drums.

UNIT 1 READING

CONCEPT
MELODY

Upward and Downward

How does the song start?

How does the song end?

All Night, All Day

 CD 10:24

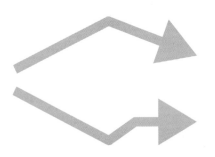

Tap the cakes at the end.

 CD 10:27 Cut the Cake

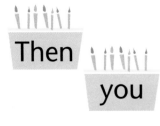

Then

you

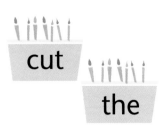

cut

the

cake.

Steady Beat and No Beat

Which pictures show steady beat?

The Wind Blew East

CD 10:31

Longer and Shorter

Which pictures show a long sound?
Which pictures show a short sound?

 CD 10:35

Hunt the Cows

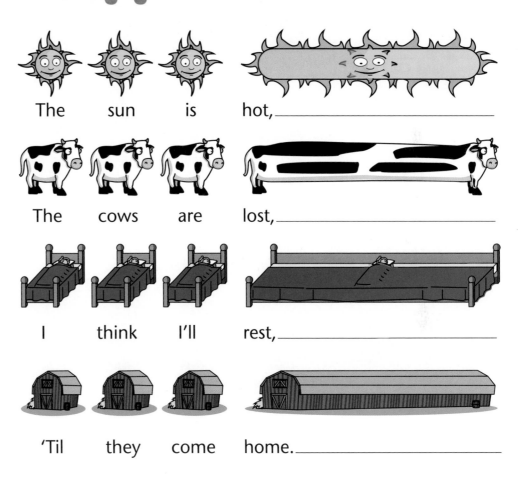

The sun is hot,_____

The cows are lost,_____

I think I'll rest,_____

'Til they come home._____

Listen and move to show long and short.

 **LISTENING** CD 11:1

Laideronette
by Maurice Ravel

83

More Long and Short Sounds

Find longer and shorter sounds.

This Little Light of Mine

CD 11:2

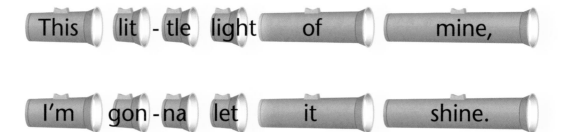

This | lit - tle | light | of | mine,

I'm | gon - na | let | it | shine.

LISTENING CD 11:5

Sleight of Feet
by Hershy Kay

Listen for long and short sounds.

Higher and Lower

Move your arms up high for higher pitches.

Touch the floor for lower pitches.

A la rueda rueda
'Round and 'Round

CD 11:6

LISTENING CD 11:10

C-A-G
by Billy Taylor

C

G A

One and Two Sounds to a Beat

Sing and pat with the beat.
Tap with the words.

CD 11:11

Seesaw

| See | - | saw | up | and | down, |

| In | the | air | and | on | the | ground. |

Compare the wagons and the seesaws.

 **LISTENING** CD 11:14

The Wagon Passes
by Edward Elgar

Listen and tap the wagons.

Time for Rhythm

Which shows one sound to a beat?

Which shows two sounds to a beat?

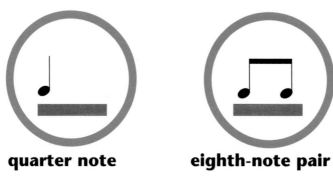

quarter note   eighth-note pair

Clap and say the words in rhythm.

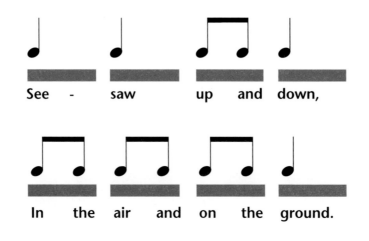

See - saw   up   and down,

In   the   air   and   on   the   ground.

LISTENING CD 11:16

Grasshopper's Wedding
by Béla Bartók

Listen and tap the rhythm.

More Fun with ♩ ♫

Clap the rhythms as you sing.

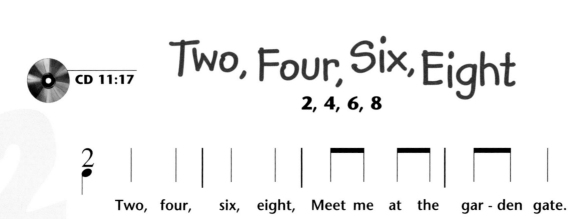

CD 11:17

Two, four, six, eight, Meet me at the gar-den gate.

If I'm late, don't wait. Two, four, six, eight.

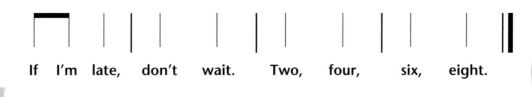

clap,   clap,   clap your   hands

 CD 11:20

Clap Your Hands

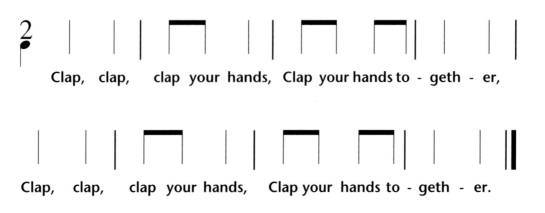

Clap, clap, clap your hands, Clap your hands to - geth - er,

Clap, clap, clap your hands, Clap your hands to - geth - er.

So and Mi

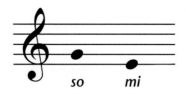

so   mi

Sing pitches with hand signs.

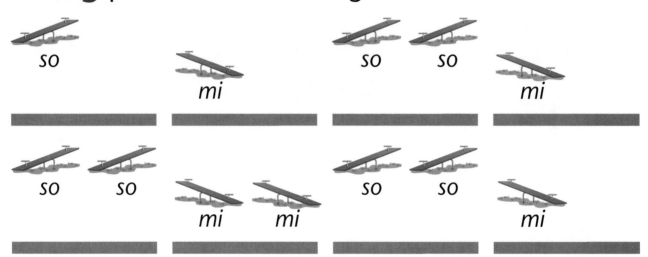

so

mi

so   so

mi

so   so

mi   mi

so   so

mi

Sing the song with words.

Seesaw

CD 11:11

American Song

See - saw   up   and down,

In   the   air   and   on   the   ground.

Practice Pitches

Name the pitches.
Sing the song, but whisper the notes with x on them.
Which part is softer?

TWO, FOUR, SIX, EIGHT
2, 4, 6, 8

CD 11:17

English Nursery Rhyme
Music by Marilyn Copeland Davidson

Two, four, six, eight.

Meet me at the gar - den gate.

If I'm late, don't wait.

Two, four, six, eight.

Find *So* and *Mi*

Find *so* and *mi* in this song.
Sing with hand signs.

Bee, Bee, Bumblebee

CD 11:24

American Rhyme
Music by Marilyn Copeland Davidson

Bee, bee, bum - ble - bee,

Stung a man up - on his knee,

Stung a pig up - on his snout,

I de - clare that you are out.

Use What You Know

Sing and play with *so* and *mi*.

Here We Sit

CD 11:27

American Singing Game

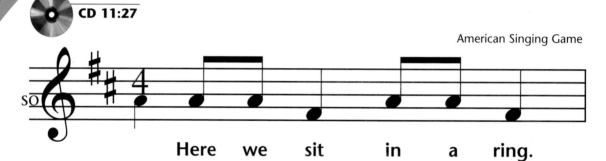

Here we sit in a ring.

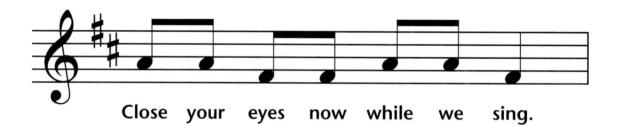

Close your eyes now while we sing.

One of us will go and hide.

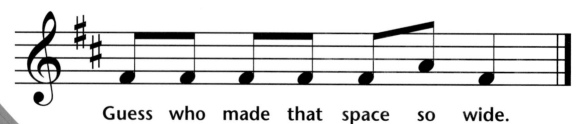

Guess who made that space so wide.

Sing with *La*

la   so   mi

Find *mi, so,* and **?** in the song.

Snail, Snail

CD 11:31

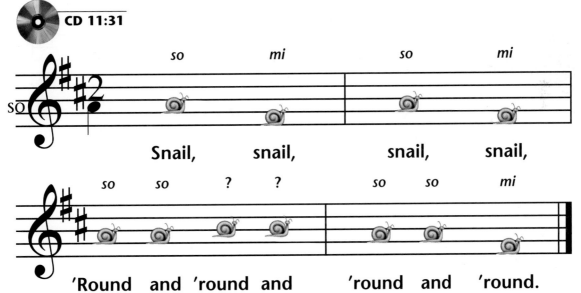

so   mi   so   mi

Snail,   snail,   snail,   snail,

so   so   ?   ?   so   so   mi

'Round and 'round and   'round and 'round.

Is the new pitch higher or lower
than *so*?

Play a snail game.

93

Practice with *La*

Find *la*.
Read the pitches.

Lucy Locket

CD 11:34

American Folk Song

so

Lu - cy Lock - et lost her pock - et,

Kit - ty Fish - er found it.

Not a pen - ny was there in it,

On - ly rib - bon 'round it.

No Sound on a Beat

Happiness
A.A. Milne

CD 11:37

John   had   Great   Big   Water- proof   Boots   on;

John   had a   Great   Big   Water- proof   Hat;

John   had a   Great   Big

Water-   proof   Mackin-   tosh—And

that   (said   John)   is

that.

Quarter Rest

𝄽 means no sound on a beat.
Find the 𝄽 in the song.

Pease Porridge Hot

CD 11:38

English Nursery Rhyme

1. Pease   por - ridge   hot,
2. Some   like   it   hot,

Pease   por - ridge   cold.
Some   like   it   cold.

Pease   por - ridge   in   the   pot
Some   like   it   in   the   pot

Nine   days   old.

Practice with ⁊

Find the ⁊ and then sing the song.

A *Mi-So-La* Melody

Read the pitches and rhythms.

Arre, mi burrito

Gid'yup, Little Burro

CD 12:5

Latin American Folk Song
English words by MMH

Spanish: A - rre, mi bu - rri - to, que
English: Gid - 'yup, lit - tle *bur - ro,* we're

va - mos a Be - lén.
go - ing to *Be - lén,*

Que ma - ña-na es fies - ta y el
Fies - *ta* is to - mor - row, and

o - tro tam - bién.
next day a - gain.

98

Fun with Pitches

Find the leaps in the song.

Sing and name the yellow pitches.

Star Light, Star Bright

CD 12:9

Traditional

Use What You Know

CD 12:13

Traditional Children's Song

Rain, rain, go a - way.

Come a - gain some oth - er day.

Rain, rain, go a - way.

Lit - tle chil - dren want to play.

Clap and say this rhythm with the song.

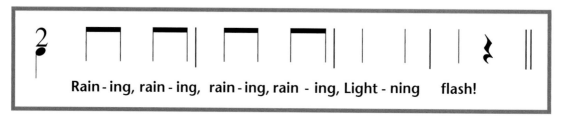

Rain - ing, rain - ing, rain - ing, rain - ing, Light - ning flash!

Mi-So-La and Rhythms You Know

Sing this *mi-so-la* song about geese.

Kari

Wild Geese

CD 12:20

Japanese Folk Song
English Words by
Florence White and Kazuo Akiyama

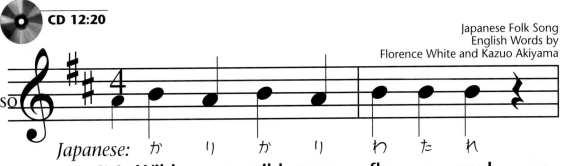

Japanese: か り か り わ た れ
English: Wild geese, wild geese, fly a - way!

おおき な か り は さ き に
Big goose a-head of you leads the way,

ちぃ さ な か り は あ と に
Small geese be-hind as you fly a - way.

な か よ く わ た れ
Peace - ful - ly, peace - ful - ly fly a - way.

101

AB Form

Listen and follow the AB form.

LISTENING CD 12:27

Bourrée
by George Frideric Handel

Listening Map for *Bourrée*

One, Two, Three, Four, Five

1,2,3,4,5

CD 12:28

American Game Song

One, two, three, four, five.

Once I caught a fish a - live.

Six, sev - en, eight, nine, ten.

Then I let him go a - gain.

Solo 1

Solo 2

Why did you let it go? Be -
Which fin - ger did it bite? The

cause it bit my fin - ger so!
lit - tle fin - ger on my right!

103

Spotlight on Performance

Spotlight on Performance

Songs to Perform

Stories to Perform

CONCEPT
RHYTHM

Grasshoppers rub their legs together to make noise. It sounds like they are playing an instrument.

Grasshoppers Three

CD 13:19

American Folk Song

Grass-hop-pers three   a - fid - dl - ing went,

Hey,   ho,   nev - er   be   still!

They   paid   no   mo - ney toward their   rent,

THE LOCUST

Locust, locust, playing a flute,
Locust, locust, playing a flute!
Away up on the pine-tree bough,
    Playing a flute,
    Playing a flute!

—Poem from the Zuñi People

Zuñi grasshopper carving

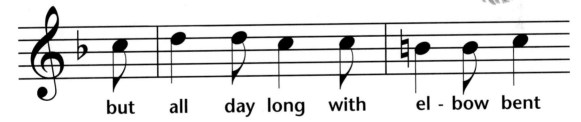

but   all   day long with   el - bow bent

They fid-dled a tune called Ril - la - by - ril - la - by,

Fid-dled a tune called Ril - la - by - rill.

CONCEPT
MELODY

Mary's little lamb is silly!
How does it get in trouble?

Mary's Coal Black Lamb

CD 13:22

American Song
Words by Ken Foy

1. Mar - y had a lit - tle lamb,

lit - tle lamb, lit - tle lamb.

Mar - y had a lit - tle lamb,

its fleece was black as coal.

2. 'Cause ev'rywhere that Mary went,
Mary went, Mary went,
Ev'rywhere that Mary went ,
the lamb kept falling in a big mud hole!

If All the World Were Paper

CD 13:41

English Folk Song

If all the world were pa - per

and all the sea were ink,

if all the trees were bread and cheese,

what would we ev - er drink?

CONCEPT
MELODY

Na Bahia Tem
In Bahia Town

 CD 13:44

Brazilian Folk Song
English Version by Ruth De Cesare

Portuguese: Na Ba - hi - a tem,
English: In Ba - hi - a town

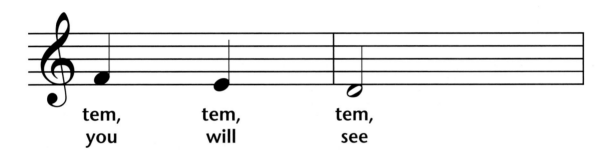

tem, tem, tem,
you will see

na Ba - hi - a tem mo - re - na,
there's a dark - haired girl and pen - ny

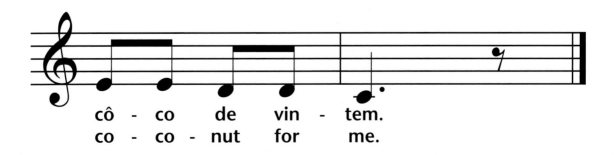

cô - co de vin - tem.
co - co - nut for me.

2. Oh I walked and walked in the sea,
   Looking for a needle but a thimble's all I see.

CONCEPT
MELODY

This Old Man

CD 14:18

English Game Song

1. This old man, he played one;
2. This old man, he played two;
3. This old man, he played three;

He played knick-knack on my thumb.
He played knick-knack on my shoe.
He played knick-knack on my knee.

With a knick-knack, pad-dy whack,

Give a dog a bone;

This old man came roll-ing home.

4. four; door	8. eight; gate
5. five; hive	9. nine; spine
6. six; sticks	10. ten; once again
7. seven; up to heaven	

CONCEPT
RHYTHM

This song is a lullaby.
It comes from Mozambique.
Mozambique is a country in Africa.

CD 14:21 **Yo, Mamana, Yo**
Oh, Mama, Oh

Tsonga Folk Song

Tsonga: **Yo,** ma - ma - na, yo,
English: **Oh,** ma - ma, _____ oh,

Yo, ma - ma - na, yo,
Oh, ma - ma, _____ oh.

Un - ga fam - ba u - ni si - ya.
Oh, if on - ly you were here now,

U - ni si - ye - la vusi - wa - na.
I could fall a - sleep once a - gain.

Read this poem.

Play the instruments after you read two lines of the poem.

Jump or Jiggle

Frogs jump
Caterpillars hump

Worms wiggle
Bugs jiggle

Rabbits hop
Horses clop

Snakes slide
Sea gulls glide

Mice creep
Deer leap

Puppies bounce
Kittens pounce

Lions stalk–
But–
I walk!

—*Evelyn Beyer*

The Rabbit in the Moon

Folktale from Japan

One day the Man-in-the-Moon looked down from the sky.

He saw Fox, Rabbit, and Monkey playing in the forest.

The Man-in-the-Moon wondered which animal was the kindest. He decided to find out. He left the moon and dressed in old clothes to fool them.

"I am hungry," the old man said.
"Please help me."

Fox found a fish that
was fat and floppy.

Monkey found fruit and
hummed him a song.

But Rabbit found nothing.

Rabbit asked Fox and Monkey to make him a campfire. "You can cook me," Rabbit said to the man. "I will be your dinner."

The Man-in-the-Moon smiled at Rabbit. "Rabbit, you are the kindest," he said. "Don't cook yourself for me. Come with me to the moon."

So Rabbit went with the Man-in-the-Moon to live on the moon. If you look closely, you might see them!

CONCEPT
RHYTHM

Why the Beetle Has a Gold Coat

Folktale from Brazil

Once there was a brown beetle walking down a path.

A paca raced by him to the end of the path and back.

"Did you see that?" the paca asked the beetle.

"Yes," said the beetle. "You are very fast."

"I bet you are slower than a snail," laughed the paca.

A parrot was watching nearby.

He said, "Why don't you race to find out? I will make a gold coat for the winner."

The paca and the beetle agreed to race.

The parrot said, "On your mark. Get set. Go!"

The paca ran past the beetle and was gone.

The paca ran as fast as he could.
But when he reached the end,
the beetle was waiting for him.

"How did you run so fast?" cried
the paca.

"You didn't say I had to run,
so I flew," laughed the beetle.

The parrot gave the beetle
a gold coat for winning.
And that is why the beetle
has a gold coat.

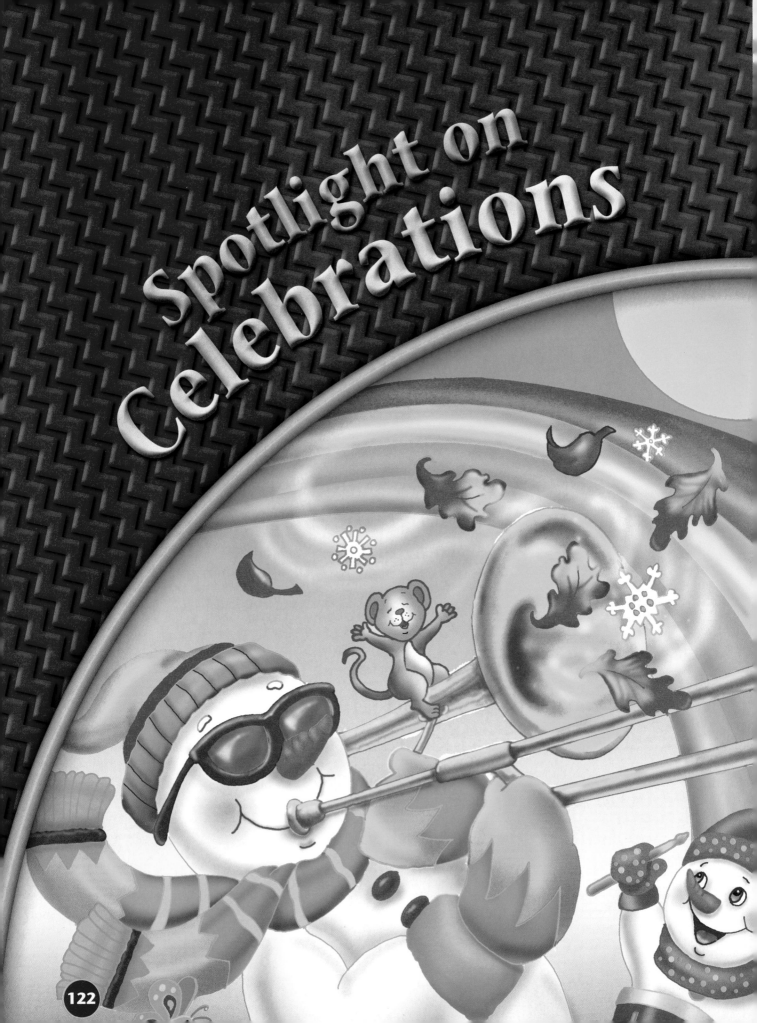

Spotlight on Celebrations

Songs of Our Country

CD 15:15

Words by Samuel F. Smith
Music by Henry Carey

My country 'tis of thee,
Sweet land of liberty,
Of thee I sing.

Land where my fathers died,
Land of the Pilgrim's pride,
From ev'ry mountain side
Let freedom ring.

Sing "America" to show
love for your country.

Pat with the steady beat.

When the Flag Goes By

CD 15:18

Words and Music by Lynn Freeman Olson

1. When the flag goes by, hold it high!
2. When you hear this song, sing out strong!

Wave it for our coun - try!
sing it for our coun - try!

When the flag goes by, hold it high!
When you hear this song, sing out strong!

And cheer when the flag goes by!
And cheer when the flag goes by!

Seasonal Songs

The wind blows in autumn.

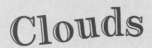

Clouds

White sheep, white sheep,
On a blue hill,
When the wind stops,
You all stand still.

When the wind blows,
You walk away slow.
White sheep, white sheep,
Where do you go?

—*Christina Rossetti*

Leaves spread everywhere
when the wind blows.

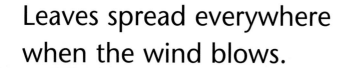

Anonymous

Au - tumn leaves are fall - ing,

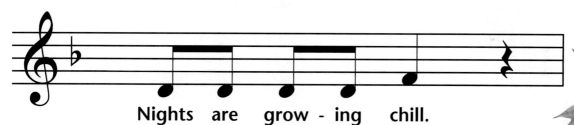

Nights are grow - ing chill.

Ma - ple leaves are turn - ing red

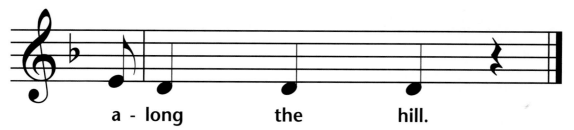

a - long the hill.

Hispanic Heritage Month is celebrated in the fall. Hispanic Americans get together to celebrate.

CD 16:1

Play the Bugle

Mexican Folk Song

Clap with the steady beat.

El vaquerito

Mexican Folk Song

The Spanish word for little cowboy is *vaquerito.*

Listen to the violins in the song.

CONCEPT
BEAT

Halloween is a time for carving pumpkins and dressing up.

 LISTENING CD 16:6

Funeral March of a Marionette

by Charles Gounod

Pat with the steady beat.

Listening Map for
Funeral March of a Marionette

Seasonal Songs

What is your favorite game in the winter?

 **LISTENING** CD 16:26

The Skaters' Waltz

by Emil Waldteufel

Use your hands to skate to the music.

Listening Map for
The Skaters' Waltz

Hanukkah is the festival of lights. It lasts for eight days.

S'vivon Sov

Dreidel Spin

Jewish Folk Song

CD 16:33

Listen to find how many days Hanukkah lasts.

A *dreidel* is a top. Children play with dreidels during Hanukkah.

Dreidel Song

Twirl about, dance about,
    Spin, spin, spin!
Turn, Dreidel, turn—
    Time to begin!

Soon it is Hanukkah—
    Fast, Dreidel, fast!
For you will lie still
    When Hanukkah's past.

—*Efraim Rosenzweig*

CONCEPT
BEAT

Christmas is a time for singing carols.

Jolly Old Saint Nicholas

CD 17:8

American Carol

1. Jol - ly old Saint Nich - o - las,
2. When the clock is strik - ing twelve,

Lean your ear this way!
When I'm fast a - sleep,

Don't you tell a sin - gle soul
Down the chim - ney broad and black,

What I'm go - ing to say;
with your pack you'll creep.

Tap and then clap with the
steady beat.

CONCEPT
TONE COLOR

Kwanzaa is a holiday that lasts for seven days. Families and friends tell stories, sing, and dance.

LISTENING CD 17:29

Le Serpent
by Guem

Guem's family is from West Africa. "Le Serpent" means the snake.

Name the instrument you hear in "Le Serpent."

People set a beautiful
table for Kwanzaa.

Dr. Martin Luther King, Jr. wanted all people to get along.

Martin Luther King

CD 18:1 by Theresa Fullbright

Dr. Martin Luther King, Jr. wanted all people to be treated fairly.

 LISTENING CD 18:4

Everybody Oughta Know
African American Song
Collected by Sweet Honey in The Rock

This song tells about freedom, justice, and happiness.

People in China like to celebrate the New Year. They visit family and friends.

It ends with the Lantern Festival.

Go A Tin
Lantern Song

CD 18:9

Taiwanese Folk Song
English Version by MMH

English: **Lan - tern bright,   lan - tern bright,**

Light   the__ way,   my__   lan - tern bright.

143

Valentines are for special friends.

My Valentine

I have a little valentine
That someone sent to me.
It's pink and white and red and blue,
And pretty as can be.
Forget-me-nots are round the edge,
And tiny roses, too;
And such a lovely piece of lace—
The very palest blue.

And in the center there's a heart
As red as red can be!
And on it's written all in gold,
"To you, with Love from Me."

—*Mary Catherine Parsons*

Viva Valentine!

CD 18:13

by Teresa Jennings

Tap with the steady beat.

Seasonal Songs

After the cold winter has passed, it is time for spring!

Tako No Uta

The Kite Song

Japanese Folk Song

CD 18:25

Pat and clap with the steady beat.

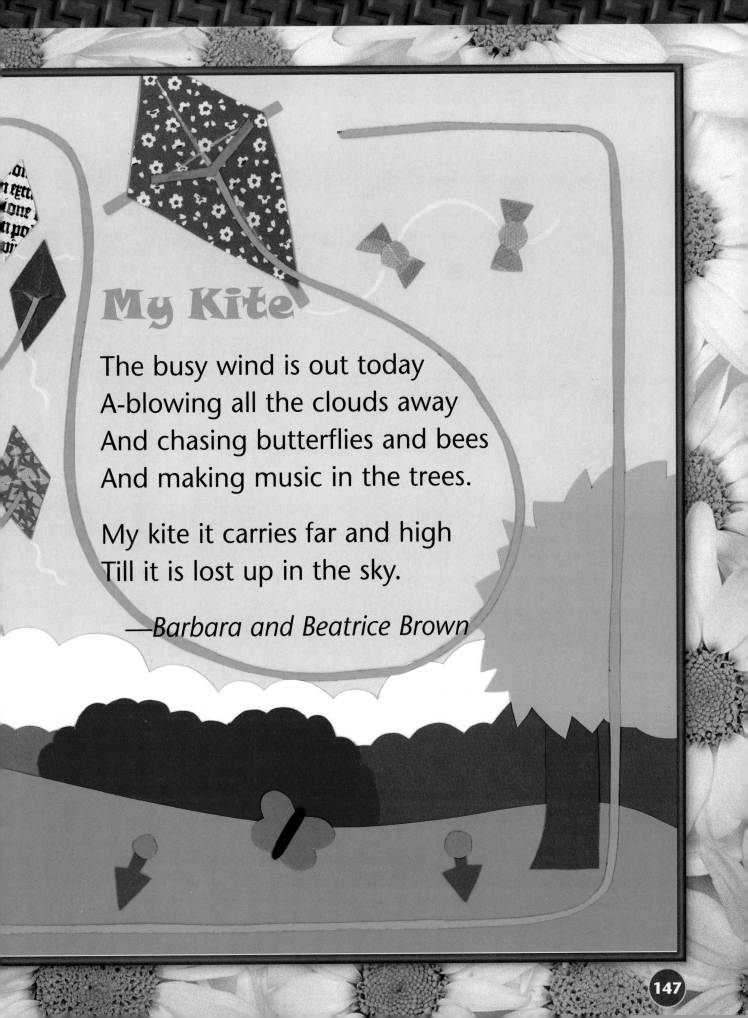

My Kite

The busy wind is out today
A-blowing all the clouds away
And chasing butterflies and bees
And making music in the trees.

My kite it carries far and high
Till it is lost up in the sky.

—*Barbara and Beatrice Brown*

Seasonal Songs

Summer is a time for fun.

 Art Gallery

Hourtide

by Edward Henry Potthast

Summertime
by George Gershwin

What do you like to
do in the summer?

Strings

double bass
CD 19:7

cello, 75
CD 19:6

viola, 75
CD 19:5

violin, 5, 6, 75
CD 19:4

Woodwinds

bassoon, 53
CD 19:15

oboe, 52
CD 19:13

clarinet, 52
CD 19:12

flute, 29

CD 19:10

tuba, 29
CD 19:22

Brass

trombone
CD 19:21

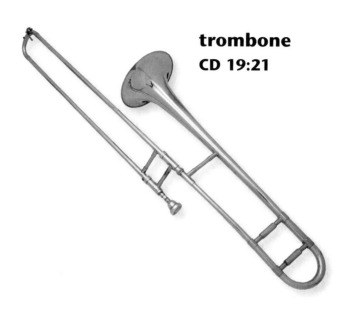

French horn, 53
CD 19:20

trumpet, 80
CD 19:18

Percussion

timpani, 53
CD 19:26

triangle, 36
CD 19:34

xylophone, 55
CD 19:30

glockenspiel, 55
CD 19:29

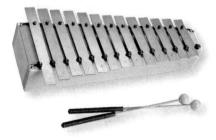

maracas, 36
CD 20:35

mbira, 74
CD 20:6

CREDITS

Illustration Credits: Winky Adam: 146, 147. Susan Aiello: 36, 37. Martha Avilés: 22, 23. Kristin Barr: 16, 17. Shirley Beckes: 34, 35. Karen Bell: 42. Rose Mary Berlin: 56, 57. Ken Bowse: 137. Robin Boyer: 85. Vicki Bradley: 108, 109. Nan Brooks: 119, 120, 121. Priscilla Burris: 132. Carly Castillon: 068–069. Jayoung Cho: 24, 25. Emilie Chollat: vi, 104, 105. Carolyn Croll: 76, 77. Liz Goulet Dubois: 111. Janet Louise Ecklebarger: 14, 15, 38, 39, 56, 57. Kathi Ember: 18, 19, 116, 118. Rusty Fletcher: 44. Felipe Galindo: 49. Mariano Gil: v, 78, 79. Greg Harris: 47. Steve Henry: 58. Nathan Young Jarvis: 110. Karol Kaminsk: 76. Carol Koeller: 63. Fran Lee: 70, 71. Monica Lee: 14, 15. Stephen Lewis: 114, 115. Loretta Lustig: 50, 51. Heather Maione: 46, 47. Elise Mills: 130. Susan Nethery: 21. Kathy O'Malley: iv, 10, 11. Philomena O'Neill: 30. Page O'Rourke: 60, 61. Laura Ovresat: 12, 13. Paula Pertile: 52, 53. Ruth Rivers: 40, 41. Aaron Romo: 71. Janet K. Skiles: 1, 122, 123. Susan Swan: 28, 29. Nicole Tadgell: 112. Mike Tofanelli: 72, 73. Janee Trasler: 26, 27. Kathy Wilburn: 62. Jason Wolff: 106, 107.

Photography Credits:
All photographs are copyright of Macmillan/McGraw-Hill (MMH) except as noted below.

Allan Landau for MMH: iv–vii: t.r., 22: l., r., 36: t.l., t.r., 37: b.c.l., b.c.r., b.l., b.r., t.c.l., t.c.r., t.l., t.r., 38: c., l., r., 43: b.l., 55: b., 59: b., c., t., 63: t., 115: c.r. Jade Albert for MMH: cover, i: b.r. Jim Powell for MMH: 36: b.c.l., 75: t.c.l., t.l., t.r., 129: l. Shane Morgan for MMH: 66: l., r.

iv–vii: b.c., b.l.c., b.c.r., b.l., c.l., t.c., t.l. PhotoDisc, Inc.; b.r., c.r., t.r. Corbis. 2: b.l., c.l. Image Club Graphics; r., t.l. Corbis. 2–3: b. PhotoDisc, Inc. 3: c.r.,

t.r. PhotoDisc, Inc.; t.c.l. Diamar; t.c.r., t.l. Image Club Graphics. 4: b. Owaki-Kulla/Corbis. 5: b.l. Chuck Keeler, Jr./Corbis; b.r. Michael Keller/Corbis; t.l. Corbis; t.r. David Zimmerman/ Corbis. 7: b.r. George Shelley/ Corbis; c.r. Ronnie Kaufman/ Corbis; l. Corbis; t.r. Richard Hutchings/Corbis. 8: r. Eleanora Ghioldi/Corbis; t. Steve Chenn/ Corbis. 9: b. Jerry Tobias/Corbis; c. Ariel Skelley/Corbis. 17: b.r. Edward Hicks/Art Resource, NY. 21: b.r. Burstein Collection/ Corbis. 25: c.l. Corbis; c.r. Premium Stock/Corbis; l. Steve & Dave Maslowski/Photo Researchers, Inc.; r. Tony Freeman/PhotoEdit, Inc. 26–27: t. PhotoDisc, Inc. 28: t.l. D. Robert Franz & Lorri Franz/ Corbis. 29: r. PhotoDisc, Inc. 31: b.l. Nancy R. Cohen/PhotoDisc Green/Getty Images; b.r. PhotoDisc, Inc./Getty Images; t.l. Myrleen Ferguson Cate/ PhotoEdit, Inc.; t.r. Lisette Le Bon/SuperStock, Inc. 32: l., r. Ellen McCullough Brabson. 32–33: bkgd. George H. H. Huey/Corbis. 33: b., t. Ellen McCullough Brabson. 34–35: t. Comstock. 40: bkgd. Corel. 40–41: t. Corel. 41: bkgd. Corel. 47: b. Roger Tidman/ Corbis. 52: c.l. PhotoDisc, Inc. 53: c., l., r. PhotoDisc, Inc. 54: b. Arne Hodalic/Corbis; c. Hideo Haga/HAGA/The Image Works. 54–55: t. Peter Hendrie/Getty Images. 56–57: bkgd. Corel. 64: b.r. Erich Lessing/Art Resource, Inc. 65: c.r. Corbis. 67: c. Diego Rivera: Banco de Mexico Trust/ Schalkwijk/Art Resource, NY. 74: b.l. Paul Novitski/Dandemutande; t.c. Fred and MyLinda King; t.l. PhotoDisc, Inc.; t.r. Jason Lauré. 75: b.l. Wladimir Polak/Lebrecht Music Collection. 77: r. Corbis. 80: b. PhotoDisc, Inc. 83: b.r. PhotoDisc, Inc. 86: b. PhotoDisc, Inc. 91: b.r. PhotoDisc, Inc. 94: b.r. Image Club Graphics. 95: t.r. Corbis. 96: PhotoDisc, Inc. 98: t.r. PhotoDisc, Inc. 101:

r. PhotoDisc, Inc. 103: l. MetaCreations/Kai Power Photos; r. MetaTools. 106: t.l. Jim Richardson/Corbis. 107: t.c.r. Florentino Martinez/ Wright's Indian Art. 111: b., r. PhotoDisc, Inc. 113: r. Larry Luxner/Luxner News, Inc. 113: t. Corbis. 114: b.c.l., b.r. PhotoDisc, Inc. 115: conga, vibraslap, PhotoDisc, Inc. 124: c. MetaCreations/Kai Power Photos; r. PhotoDisc, Inc. 124–125: bkgd. PhotoDisc, Inc. 126: c., r. PhotoDisc, Inc. 126–127: bkgd., leaves, PhotoDisc, Inc. 128: c., r. PhotoDisc, Inc.; l. Image Club Graphics. 129: r. PhotoDisc, Inc. 130–131: bkgd. PhotoDisc, Inc. 132–133: bkgd. Corbis. 133: t. PhotoDisc, Inc. 134: l. PhotoDisc, Inc. 135: b.l. Image Club Graphics; b.r. Brand X/ Getty Images; c., t.l. PhotoDisc, Inc.; t.r. PNC/Getty Images. 136–137: bkgd. PhotoDisc, Inc. 138–139: c. Chester Higgins Jr./Photo Researchers, Inc. 140: b. AP/Wide World Photos; t. SuperStock, Inc. 141: b. Leon Morris/Redferns Music Picture Library. 142: c. Peter/Georgina Bowater/Mira.com. 142–143: bkgd. MetaCreations/Kai Power Photos. 143: b.r. SuperStock, Inc. 144–145: bkgd. MetaCreations/Kai Power Photos. 146–147: bkgd. PhotoDisc, Inc. 148: b.c. PhotoDisc, Inc. 148: b.l. Artville; b.r. PhotoDisc, Inc.; t. Art Resource, Inc. 148–149: bkgd. MetaCreations/Kai Power Photos; bkgd. PhotoDisc, Inc. 149: b. PhotoDisc, Inc.; c. Artville; t. Comstock. 150: c.r., t.l., t.r. PhotoDisc, Inc. 151: b.l. PhotoDisc, Inc. 153: r. PhotoDisc, Inc.

All attempts have been made to provide complete and correct credits by the time of publication.

ACKNOWLEDGMENTS

Literature

Dreidel Song, by Efraim Rosenzweig, from *Now We Begin,* by Marian J. and Efraim M. Rosenzweig. Copyright © 1937. Union of American Hebrew Congregations. Reprinted in *The Arbuthnot Anthology of Children's Literature.* Compiled by May Hill Arbuthnot. Copyright © 1961 by Scott, Foresman, and Company. All Rights Reserved.

Happiness, by A.A. Milne, from *When We Were Very Young.* Copyright © 1924, Copyright renewal by A.A. Milne, © 1952. Published by E.P. Dutton. All Rights Reserved.

Jump or Jiggle, by Evelyn Beyer, from *Another Here and Now Storybook,* by Lucy Sprague Mitchell, Copyright 1937 by E.P Dutton, renewed © 1965 by Lucy Sprague Mitchell. Used by permission of Dutton Children's Books, A Division of Penguin Young Readers Group, A Member of Penguin Group (USA) Inc., 345 Hudson Street, New York, NY 10014. All rights reserved.

My Kite, by Barbara and Beatrice Brown. Courtesy The Christian Science Publishing Society, Boston, MA. Reprinted in *Read-Together Poems,* tested, selected, and arranged by Helen A. Brown and Harry J. Heltman. Harper & Row, Publishers, Inc., Copyright © 1949, 1961. All Rights Reserved.

My Valentine, by Mary Catherine Parsons. Reprinted in *Read-Together Poems.* Tested, selected, and arranged by Helen A. Brown and Harry J. Heltman. Harper & Row, Publishers, Inc. Copyright © 1949, 1961. All Rights Reserved.

Why the Beetle Has a Gold Coat, by Barbara Baumgartner, from *Good as Gold: Stories of Values from Around the World.* Published by Family Learning, Southland Boulevard, Orlando, FL 32809, Copyright © 1998 Dorling Kindersley Limited. All Rights Reserved.

Alphabetical Index

🎤 Interview

💿 INDEX OF SONGS AND SPEECH PIECES

Alphabetical Index

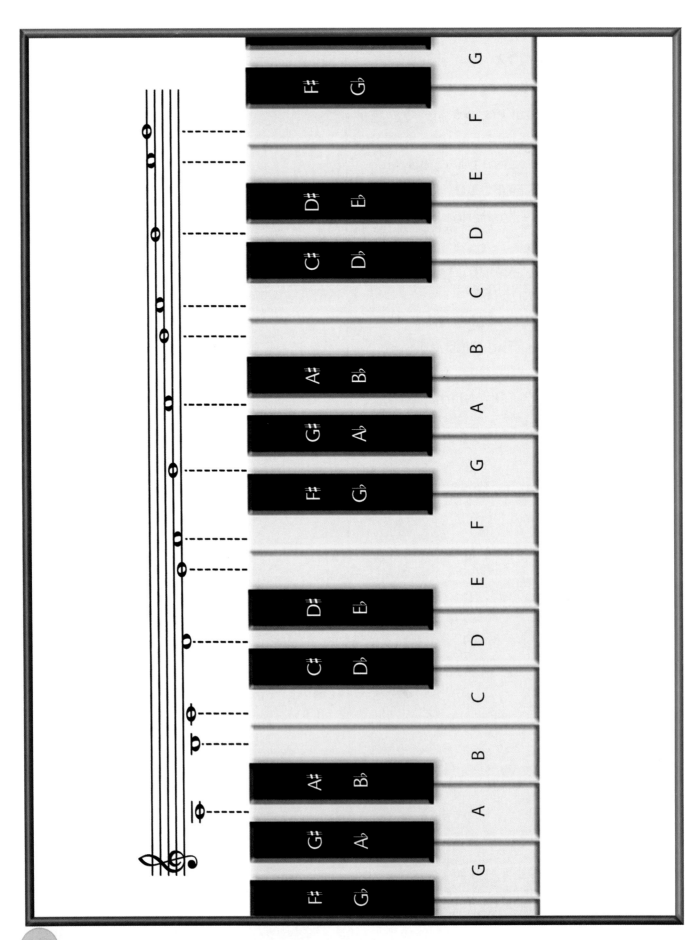